FIGHTING TERMS

Fighting Terms

THOM GUNN

FABER AND FABER

24 Russell Square

London

First published in mcmliv
by the Fantasy Press
This edition with revisions
first published in mcmlxii
second impression mcmlxvi
by Faber and Faber Limited
24 Russell Square London WC1
Printed in Great Britain by
The Bowering Press Plymouth

TO MIKE KITAY

CONTENTS

THE WOUND

The huge wound in my head began to heal
About the beginning of the seventh week.
Its valleys darkened, its villages became still:
For joy I did not move and dared not speak;
Not doctors would cure it, but time, its patient skill.

And constantly my mind returned to Troy.
After I sailed the seas I fought in turn
On both sides, sharing even Helen's joy
Of place, and growing up—to see Troy burn—
As Neoptolemus, that stubborn boy.

I lay and rested as prescription said.
Manoeuvred with the Greeks, or sallied out
Each day with Hector. Finally my bed
Became Achilles' tent, to which the lout
Thersites came reporting numbers dead.

I was myself: subject to no man's breath:
My own commander was my enemy.
And while my belt hung up, sword in the sheath,
Thersites shambled in and breathlessly
Cackled about my friend Patroclus' death.

I called for armour, rose, and did not reel.
But, when I thought, rage at his noble pain
Flew to my head, and turning I could feel
My wound break open wide. Over again
I had to let those storm-lit valleys heal.

HERE COME THE SAINTS

Here come the saints: so near, so innocent,
They gravely cross the field of moonlit snow;
We villagers gape humbly at the show.
No act or gesture can suggest intent.
They only wait until the first cock crow
Batters our ears, and with abrupt and violent
Motions into the terrible dark wood they go.

TO HIS CYNICAL MISTRESS

And love is then no more than a compromise?
An impermanent treaty waiting to be signed
    By the two enemies?
While the calculating Cupid feigning impartial-blind
Drafts it, promising peace, both leaders wise
To his antics sign but secretly double their spies.

On each side is the ignorant animal nation,
Jostling friendly in streets, enjoying in good faith
    This celebration,
Forgetting their enmity with cheers and drunken breath;
But for them there has not been yet amalgamation:
The leaders calmly plot assassination.

WIND IN THE STREET

The same faces, and then the same scandals
Confront me inside the talking-shop which I
Frequent for my own good. And an assistant
Points to the old cogwheels, the old handles
Set in machines which to buy would be to buy
The same faces, and then the same scandals.

I climb by the same stairs to a square attic,
Where I pause, for surely this is something new!
So square, so simple. It is new to be so simple.
Then I see the same sky through the skylight, static,
Cloudless, the same artificial toy-like blue.
The same stairs led to the same attic.

I only came, I explain, to look round.
I think that I have seen this line before.
Searching thoroughly, I did not see what I wanted.
What I wanted would have been what I found.
The assistant coos, I go to the shop door:
I only came, I explain, to look round.

I may return, meanwhile I'll look elsewhere:
My want may modify to what I have seen.
I step into the street, where I regain
The struggle with an uncommitted air,
Struggle with fluency, the state between
To which I still return who look elsewhere.

LAZARUS NOT RAISED

He was not changed. His friends around the grave
Stared down upon his greasy placid face
Bobbing on shadows; nothing it seemed could save
His body now from the sand below their wave,
The scheduled miracle not taking place.

He lay inert beneath those outstretched hands
Which beckoned him to life. Though coffin-case
Was ready to hold life and winding-bands
At his first stir would loose the frozen glands,
The scheduled miracle did not take place.

O Lazarus, distended body laid
Glittering without weight on death's surface:
Rise now before you sink, we dare not wade
Into that sad marsh where (the mourners cried)
The scheduled miracle cannot take place.

When first aroused and given thoughts and breath,
He chose to amble at his normal pace
In childhood fields imaginary and safe—
Much like the trivial territory of death
(The miracle had not yet taken place);

He chose to spend his thoughts like this at first
And disregard the nag of offered grace,
Then chose to spend the rest of them in rest.
The final effort came, forward we pressed
To see the scheduled miracle take place:

Abruptly the corpse blinked and shook his head
Then sank again, sliding without a trace

From sight, to take slime on the deepest bed
Of vacancy. He had chosen to stay dead,
The scheduled miracle did not take place.

Nothing else changed. I saw somebody peer
Stooping, into the oblong box of space.
His friends had done their best: without such fear,
Without that terrified awakening glare,
The scheduled miracle would have taken place.

LOFTY IN THE PALAIS DE DANSE

You are not random picked. I tell you you
Are much like one I knew before, that died.
Shall we sit down, and drink and munch a while
—I want to see if you will really do:
If not we'll get it over now outside.
Wary I wait for one unusual smile.

I never felt this restiveness with her:
I lay calm wanting nothing but what I had.
And now I stand each night outside the Mills
For girls, then shift them to the cinema
Or dance hall . . . Like the world, I've gone to bad.
A deadly world: for, once I like, it kills.

The same with everything: the only posting
I ever liked, was short. And so in me
I kill the easy things that others like
To teach them that no liking can be lasting:
All that you praise I take, what modesty
What gentleness, you ruin while you speak.

And partly that I couldn't if I would
Be bed-content with likenesses so dumb.
Passed in the street, they seem identical
To her original, yet understood
Exhaustively as soon as slept with, some
Lack this, some that, and none like her at all.

You praise my strength. The muscle on my arm.
Yes. Now the other. Yes, about the same.
I've got another muscle you can feel.

Dare say you knew. Only expected harm
Falls from a khaki man. That's why you came
With me and when I go you follow still.

Now that we sway here in the shadowed street
Why can't I keep my mind clenched on the job?
Your body is a good one, not without
Earlier performance, but in this repeat
The pictures are unwilled that I see bob
Out of the dark, and you can't turn them out.

ROUND AND ROUND

The lighthouse keeper's world is round,
Belongings skipping in a ring—
All that a man may want, therein,
A wife, a wireless, bread and brains,
Yet night by night his vigour strains
To ride upon the constant sound
The spinning waves make while they break
For their own endeavour's sake:
The lighthouse keeper's world is round.

He wonders, winding up the stair
To light the lamp that guides the ships,
Why each secured possession skips
With face toward the centre turned;
From table-loads of books has learned
Shore-worlds are round as well, not square,
But there things dance with faces out-
ward turned. Confronting what they doubt?
He wonders, winding up the stair.

When it is calm, the rocks are safe
To take a little exercise,
But all he does is fix his eyes
On that huge totem he has left,
Within whose curve his thoughts still drift:
The stony skeleton of himself,
Where all is jointed, all is neat.
There is a lapping at his feet
When, in a calm, the rocks are safe.

HELEN'S RAPE

Hers was the last authentic rape:
From forced content of common breeder
Bringing the violent dreamed escape
Which came to her in different shape
Than to Europa, Danae, Leda:

Paris. He was a man. And yet
That Aphrodite brought this want
Found too implausible to admit:
And so against this story set
The story of a stolen aunt.

Trust man to prevaricate and disguise
Such an event when it takes place:
And Romans stifling Sabine cries
To multiply and vulgarise
What even Trojan did with grace.

Helen herself could not through flesh
Abandon flesh: she felt it bound
Her absent body, felt afresh
The mortal context, and the mesh
Of the continual battle's sound.

THE SECRET SHARER

Over the ankles in snow and numb past pain
I stared up at my window three stories high:
From a white street unconcerned as a dead eye,
I patiently called my name again and again.

The curtains were lit, through glass were lit by doubt.
And there was I, within the room alone.
In the empty wind I stood and shouted on:
But O, what if the strange head should peer out?

Suspended taut between two equal fears
I was like to be torn apart by their strong pull:
What, I asked, if I never hear my call?
And what if it reaches my insensitive ears?

Fixed in my socket of thought I saw them move
Aside, I saw that some uncertain hand
Had touched the curtains. Mine, I wondered? And,
At this instant, the wind turned in its groove.

The wind turns in its groove and I am here
Lying in bed, the snow and street outside;
Fire-glow still reassuring; dark defied.
The wind turns in its groove: I am still there.

LA PRISONNIERE

Now I will shut you in a box
With massive sides and a lid that locks.
Only by that I can be sure
That you are still mine and mine secure,
And know where you are when I'm not by,
No longer needing to wonder and spy.
I may forget you at party or play
But do not fear I shall keep away
With any Miss Brown or any Miss Jones.
If my return finds a heap of bones—
Too dry to simper, too dry to whine—
You will still be mine and only mine.

CARNAL KNOWLEDGE

Even in bed I pose: desire may grow
More circumstantial and less circumspect
Each night, but an acute girl would suspect
My thoughts might not be, like my body, bare.
I wonder if you know, or, knowing, care?
You know I know you know I know you know.

I am not what I seem, believe me, so
For the magnanimous pagan I pretend
Substitute a forked creature as your friend.
When darkness lies—without a roll or stir—
Flaccid, you want a competent poseur
Whose seeming is the only thing to know.

I prod you, you react. Thus to and fro
We turn, to see ourselves perform the same
Comical act inside the tragic game.
Or is it perhaps simpler: could it be
A mere tear-jerker void of honesty
In which there are no motives left to know?

Lie back. Within a minute I will stow
Your greedy mouth, but will not yet to grips.
'There is a space between the breast and lips.'
Also a space between the thighs and head,
So great, we might as well not be in bed:
For we learn nothing here we did not know.

I hardly hoped for happy thoughts, although
In a most happy sleeping time I dreamt
We did not hold each other in contempt.

Then lifting from   lids night's penny weights
I saw that lack of love contaminates.
You know I know you know I know you know.

Abandon me to stammering, and go;
If you have tears, prepare to cry elsewhere—
I know of no emotion we can share.
Your intellectual protests are a bore,
And even now I pose, so now go, for
I know you know.

THE COURT REVOLT

The worst conspired, their differences sunk;
And others joined from weakness or because
Sick boredom had succeeded leisure drunk:
King stork was welcome to replace a log.
They tittered at the thrill, then hushed, agog.

Nor was this doomed king either log, or dead:
Still active, generous, striding through the court.
Suspicion never came into his head.
Not overthrown by system or idea
But individual jealousy and fear.

Yet he was doomed, and not by them alone.
—How can a man hold office in these days?
Not that it is too much for flesh and bone
But flesh and bone are far too much for it:
There needs a something inhuman to fit.

His natural magnanimity would appear
Insulting charity to the subject now.
The subject's real subjection, though, was near:
Coming from justice without face or shape
Was self-subjection which has no escape.

The loyal rescued him one night. What then?
Not write his memoirs in America,
Nor take a manual job with foreign men,
Nor fight against his country, which he loved.
His links were broken; but were scarcely proved.

Though on a larger scale, see in his case
A problem which is problem of us all:
His human flames of energy had no place—
The grate that they were lit for would not hold,
The vacant grates were destined to be cold.

THE RIGHT POSSESSOR

Bandit to prince was his advance one night,
He was soon overthrown, he was exiled.
At daybreak back the roads of his delight
He went deliberately, no longer child.
On either hand leaves withered by his shot,
But all, the weeping trees, all, he forgot.

The devastated country was enlarged,
Villages burnt to nothing, fields of wheat
Flattened, for his soldiers—now discharged—
Had trampled everything beneath their feet.
He did not look, and only checked his stride
Once, on a cartridge belt he kicked aside.

Some orphaned boys were playing in the sun
And helped the tall sad man to find his road.
These boys apart, he hated everyone
Born in this fickle land he had let blood,
And so, indignant, reached the unruined sea,
Jumped in a boat and left the country free.

The years abroad brought bad dreams, he would leap
Shuddering from bed, but seldom mix with men.
Habit of memory between sleep and sleep
Was hardening to fixed ideal, when
A message from the latest government
Recalled this exile from his banishment.

But at the frontier, how the land seemed small!
Calm, neutral, waiting, drifted deep with snow.
He noticed no one noticed him at all,

No widow's looks, no gratitude. Below
His movements set a still indifference:
Forward or backward now made equal sense.

He paced the snow, from cold not expectation,
His footprints obvious in a perfect round.
Then least suspected in that lonely station
A boy ran forward on the frozen ground
And shot the muffled stranger in the head,
Who fell upon the platform and was dead.

The news put all the nation into mourning.
What need to let my conqueror die, she cried?
Why did my contradictory mind keep warning
That loss of dignity lay at his side?
Now indecision and delay have lost
For ever what I always wanted most.

LOOKING GLASS

Remote, it lives now in a tiny glass,
Charmed-still for ever at one stage of growing·
Trees are in leaf, and children all day long
Laugh in their effortless continual going
To hidden ends along the ways of grass,
And birds make great perspectives of their song.

I still hold Eden in my garden wall.
It was not innocence lost, not innocence
But a fine callous fickleness which could fix
On every novelty the mind or sense
Reached for, gratification being all,
And closed the tool-box for the box of tricks.

I am the gardener now myself, and know,
Though I am free to leave the path and tear
Ripe from the branch the yellows and the reds,
I am responsible for order here
(The time it takes to teach the fruits to grow,
The pains of keeping neat the flower beds).

What little watering I do is pleasure,
I let the birds on pear and apple sup,
I do not use my clippers or my rake,
I do not tie the fallen branches up,
I leave the weeding and employ my leisure
In idling on the lawns or by the lake.

Gardening manuals frown at this neglect,
But risks are authorised by such a weather.
What else but water should the flowers need?

I will enjoy the green before it wither,
And do not care if villagers suspect
That my green towers sweetly go to seed.

I see myself inside a looking glass,
Framed there by shadowed trees alive with song
And fruits no sooner noticed than enjoyed;
I take it from my pocket and gaze long,
Forgetting in my pleasure how I pass
From town to town, damp-booted, unemployed.

LERICI

Shelley was drowned near here. Arms at his side
He fell submissive through the waves, and he
Was but a minor conquest of the sea:
The darkness that he met was nurse not bride.

Others make gestures with arms open wide,
Compressing in the minute before death
What great expense of muscle and of breath
They would have made if they had never died.

Byron was worth the sea's pursuit. His touch
Was masterful to water, audience
To which he could react until an end.
Strong swimmers, fishermen, explorers: such
Dignify death by thriftless violence—
Squandering all their little left to spend.

A MIRROR FOR POETS

It was a violent time. Wheels, racks, and fires
In every writer's mouth, and not mere rant.
Certain shrewd herdsmen, between twisted wires
Of penalty folding the realm, were thanked
For organizing spies and secret police
By richness in the flock, which they could fleece.

Hacks in the Fleet and nobles in the Tower:
Shakespeare must keep the peace, and Jonson's thumb
Be branded (for manslaughter), to the power
Of irons the admired Southampton's power was come.
Above all swayed the diseased and doubtful queen:
Her state canopied by the glamour of pain.

In this society the boundaries met
Of life and life, at danger; with no space
Being left between, except where might be set
That mathematical point whose time and place
Could not exist. Yet at this point they found
Arcadia, a fruitful permanent land.

The faint and stumbling crowds were dim to sight
Who had no time for pity or for terror:
Here moved the Forms, flooding like moonlight,
In which the act or thought perceived its error.
The hustling details, calmed and relevant.
Here mankind might behold its whole extent.

Here in a cave the Paphlagonian King
Crouched, waiting for his greater counterpart
Who one remove from likelihood may seem,

But several nearer to the human heart.
In exile from dimension, change by storm,
Here his huge magnanimity was born.

Yet the historians tell us, life meant less.
It was a violent time, and evil-smelling.
Jonson howled 'Hell's a grammar-school to this,'
But found renunciation well worth telling.
Winnowing with his flail of comedy
He showed coherence in society.

In street, in tavern, happening would cry
'I am myself, but part of something greater,
Find poets what that is, do not pass by,
For feel my fingers in your pia mater.
I am a cruelly insistent friend:
You cannot smile at me and make an end.'

THE BEACH HEAD

Now that a letter gives me ground at last
For starting from, I see my enterprise
Is more than application by a blast
Upon a trumpet slung beside a gate,
Security a fraud, and how unwise
Was disembarking on your Welfare State.

What should they see in you but what I see,
These friends you mention whom I do not know?
—You unsuspecting that a refugee
Might want the land complete, write in a tone
Too matter-of-fact, of small affairs below
Some minister's seduction of the Crown.

And even if they could be innocent,
They still applaud you, keep you satisfied
And occupy your time, which I resent.
Their werewolf lust and cunning are afraid
Of night-exposure in the hair, so hide
Distant as possible from my palisade.

I have my ground. A brain-sick enemy
Pacing the beach head he so plotted for
Which now seems trivial to his jealousy
And ignorance of the great important part,
I almost wish I had no narrow shore.
I seek a pathway to the country's heart.

Shall I be John a Gaunt and with my band
Of mad bloods pass in one spectacular dash,
Fighting before and after, through your land,

To issue out unharmed the farther side,
With little object other than panache
And showing what great odds may be defied?

That way achievement would at once be history:
Living inside, I would not know, the danger:
Hurry is blind and so does not brave mystery;
I should be led to underrate, by haste,
Your natural beauties: while I, hare-brained stranger,
Would not be much distinguished from the rest.

Or shall I wait and calculate my chances,
Consolidating this my inch-square base,
Picking off rival spies that tread your glances:
Then plan when you have least supplies or clothing
A pincer-move to end in an embrace,
And risk that your mild liking turn to loathing?

A KIND OF ETHICS

Old trees are witnesses:
   Their simple religion is forced into the cold,
   No intermediary gives them rules of conduct:
   All day without a minister they hold
Primitive services.

The power that they receive
   Out of the water, air and earth, can be
   Partial at best, for only on their branches
   Where leaves start from the black extremity
Can they be said to live.

The past that they have led
   Makes unapproachable and hidden sin:
   Deep in the foul confusion of their thicket,
   So dense no human being can go in,
Dry tangled twigs lie dead.

Among such broken wood
   Wild animals give birth to sharp toothed young:
   Unregenerate, they have no time for worship.
   Careless, out of a possibly bad may come
An undeniable good.

TAMER AND HAWK

I thought I was so tough,
But gentled at your hands
Cannot be quick enough
To fly for you and show
That when I go I go
At your commands.

Even in flight above
I am no longer free:
You seeled me with your love,
I am blind to other birds—
The habit of your words
Has hooded me.

As formerly, I wheel
I hover and I twist,
But only want the feel
In my possessive thought,
Of catcher and of caught
Upon your wrist.

You but half-civilize,
Taming me in this way.
Through having only eyes
For you I fear to lose,
I lose to keep, and choose
Tamer as prey.

CAPTAIN IN TIME OF PEACE

Crudely continues what has been begun
Crudely, because the crude expedient
Sets crude and final what is to be won.
Tactics commit me falsely, what I want
Is not the raising of a siege but this:
    Honour in the town at peace.

I see you bend your head by the fireplace
Softly examining your outspread hand,
A puzzled look unguarded on your face,
As if you did not fully understand.
How can I with most gentleness explain
    I will not plot my moves again?

Something I try, and yet when I express
Trite cinema endearments, all is said.
There, I think still in terms of mere success
—Success in raising up your downturned head.
Pity a lumpish soldier out of work,
    And teach him manners with a look.

And if I cannot gracefully receive
When you are generous, know that the habit
Of soldiers is to loot. So please forgive
All my inadequacy: I was fit
For peaceful living once, and was not born
    A clumsy brute in uniform.

WITHOUT A COUNTERPART

Last night I woke in fright: you were not there.
I seemed to face across a deep sad plain
Hedged at one end, a hillock in the centre.
And I was chained, to wait and starve alone,
And could not think what I was waiting for.

I lay, peering as best I could, then saw
Two reed-lined ponds, reflections of the sky.
I noticed with a shock a long volcano
Which like a third brimmed-full with darkness lay:
And knew that from its opening death would flow.

Though I could swear I had not been before
Captived or free in this eccentric scene,
I knew it well, lonely, peculiar,
Taught it maybe by some forgotten dream.
And somehow guessed that it was right to fear.

My cheek on prickly turf I waited still.
Then the ground shook. I knew the end had come.
The whole plain rose above me like a wall.
And for my prayers I only spoke your name—
All changed at once: I had undone the spell.

The bad hole in the ground no longer gaped—
The hard land round it, flexing into flesh,
Warmed me instead of swallowing me up.
It was your mouth, and all the rest your face.
Your arms still chained me as you fell asleep.

FOR A BIRTHDAY

I have reached a time when words no longer help:
Instead of guiding me across the moors
Strong landmarks in the uncertain out-of-doors,
Or like dependable friars on the Alp
Saving with wisdom and with brandy kegs,
They are gravel-stones, or tiny dogs which yelp
Biting my trousers, running round my legs.

Description and analysis degrade,
Limit, delay, slipped land from what has been;
And when we groan My Darling what we mean
Looked at more closely would too soon evade
The intellectual habit of our eyes;
And either the experience would fade
Or our approximations would be lies.

The snarling dogs are weight upon my haste,
Tons which I am detaching ounce by ounce.
All my agnostic irony I renounce
So I may climb to regions where I rest
In springs of speech, the dark before of truth:
The sweet moist wafer of your tongue I taste,
And find right meanings in your silent mouth.

INCIDENT ON A JOURNEY

One night I reached a cave: I slept, my head
Full of the air. There came about daybreak
A red-coat soldier to the mouth, who said
'I am not living, in hell's pains I ache,
    But I regret nothing.'

His forehead had a bloody wound whose streaming
The pallid staring face illuminated.
Whether his words were mine or his, in dreaming
I found they were my deepest thoughts translated.
    '*I regret nothing:*

'Turn your closed eyes to see upon these walls
A mural scratched there by an earlier man,
And coloured with the blood of animals:
Showing humanity beyond its span,
    Regretting nothing.

'No plausible nostalgia, no brown shame
I had when treating with my enemies.
And always when a living impulse came
I acted, and my action made me wise.
    And I regretted nothing.

'I as possessor of unnatural strength
Was hunted, one day netted in a brawl;
A minute far beyond a minute's length
Took from me passion, strength, and life, and all.
    But I regretted nothing.

'Their triumph left my body in the dust;
The dust and beer still clotting in my hair

When I rise lonely, will-less. Where I must
I go, and what I must I bear.
    And I regret nothing.

'My lust runs yet and is unsatisfied,
My hate throbs yet but I am feeble-limbed;
If as an animal I could have died
My death had scattered instinct to the wind,
    Regrets as nothing.'

Later I woke. I started to my feet.
The valley light, the mist already going.
I was alive and felt my body sweet,
Uncaked blood in all its channels flowing.
    I would regret nothing.

NOTE ON THE TEXT

Fighting Terms was originally published by the
Fantasy Press in 1954. I made various revisions
for an edition brought out by the Hawk's Well
Press in New York five years later. Unfortunately
many of them were scarcely improvements. This
edition, therefore, is much closer to the original
one. It differs in the following ways: I have omit-
ted two poems and moved 'Carnal Knowledge'
from the beginning to the middle; I have made
quite a few minor alterations in language and
punctuation where the earlier version was unclear;
and I have rewritten 'Round and Round'.

T. G.